# LONDON OLYMPICS
## 1908 AND 1948

### Janie Hampton

SHIRE PUBLICA

Published in Great Britain in 2011 by Shire Publications Ltd,
Midland House, West Way, Botley, Oxford OX2 0PH,
United Kingdom.
44-02 23rd Street, Suite 219, Long Island City,
NY 11101, USA.

E-mail: shire@shirebooks.co.uk    www.shirebooks.co.uk

A CIP catalogue record for this book is available from the
British Library.

Shire Library no. 622.    ISBN-13: 978 0 74780 822 0

Janie Hampton has asserted her right under the Copyright,
Designs and Patents Act, 1988, to be identified as the
author of this book.

Designed by Myriam Bell Design and typeset in Perpetua
and Gill Sans.
Printed in China through Worldprint Ltd.

11 12 13 14 15    10 9 8 7 6 5 4 3 2 1

FRONT COVER IMAGE
Marathon runners leaving Wembley Stadium on Saturday
7 August 1948. Argentinean Delfo Cabrera won the gold
medal, beating Tom Richards, a psychiatric nurse from
Tooting Bec, by 16 seconds.

TITLE PAGE IMAGE
A poster lithographed in eight colours, designed by Walter
Herz, who came from Prague to seek refuge in Britain in
1939.

CONTENTS PAGE IMAGE
The Franco-British Exhibition Stadium was the main venue
for the 1908 Olympic Games, of which Edward VII was
patron.

ACKNOWLEDGEMENTS
Thanks are due to the following people who have given
permission to use illustrations:

British Olympic Association, page 45; Estate of Tony
Butcher, page 22 (bottom); Jock Dalrymple page 35 (top);
Getty Images, cover, title page, pages 3, 4, 18, 19, 22
(top), 23, 24, 25, 26 (bottom), 27 (top), 31 (top and
bottom), 32 (top right and bottom), 33 (bottom), 37, 38,
43, 44; Helen Gordon, page 34 (top); Maurice Graham,
page 27 (bottom); Rebecca Jenkins, pages 6, 7, 8, 9, 10,
11, 12, 13, 14, 15, 16, 17, 46, 47; Lorna Lee-Price, page
29 (left); Rowing Museum, Henley-on-Thames, page 34
(bottom); Dorothy Tyler, page 35 (bottom); Jenny
Williams, page 32 (left).

If any copyright owners have been left out, we will be
pleased to remedy the situation in the next edition.

Shire Publications is supporting the Woodland Trust, the UK's leading woodland conservation charity, by funding the dedication of trees.

# CONTENTS

# INTRODUCTION

T HE FIRST OLYMPIC GAMES that we know about were held in Greece in 776 BC and the Olympics continued every four years for the next thousand years until a Roman emperor stopped them in AD 385. About 1,500 years later, a French aristocrat, Pierre de Coubertin, held a meeting in France in 1892 to plan the revival of the ancient Olympic Games. 'My feeling is that the more you bring people together for something in which they take a special interest,' he said, 'the more it leads to increasing friendship.' De Coubertin hoped that the Olympic movement would 'contribute to building a peaceful and better world by educating youth through sport, practised without discrimination of any kind. The Olympic spirit requires mutual understanding; and friendship, solidarity and fair play.' His Olympics would

be more than an athletics event. 'Blending sport with culture and education, *Olympism* seeks to create a way of life based on the joy found in effort, the educational value of good example and respect for fundamental ethical principles.' Agreeing on those ethical principles would test the whole world's desire for peaceful effort and education.

Baron de Coubertin was inspired by the Victorian ideals of gentlemanly amateurism, fair play and muscular Christianity, as expressed in the poet Sir Henry Newbolt's line, 'Play up and play the game'. England had already shown its support for the Olympics: every year since 1850 the town of Much Wenlock in Shropshire had organised 'Olympic Games', and the racecourse was renamed the 'Olympian Fields' for the day. The townsfolk played football, cricket, held a blindfold wheelbarrow race and gave the fastest old woman a prize of a pound of tea.

After much planning, the first modern Olympic Games were held in Athens in 1896. The King of Greece paid for the restoration of the stadium, and the forty-three events included swimming, athletics, fencing and gymnastics. (The rowing had to be cancelled because of rough weather at sea.) Most of the 260 competitors were Greek, though six Britons participated. A Mr L. Elliot won the weightlifting gold and also took part in wrestling, the 100-yard dash and rope-climbing.

Discus-throwing was included, though nobody in the nineteenth century had ever seen a discus before, nor knew how to throw it. Ancient Greek statues were examined, and a good, but incorrect, guess was made. George Robertson threw the discus for Britain, sent daily reports back to *The Field* and competed at lawn tennis, though he confessed to barely knowing the rules. He also recited his own Olympic ode in the ancient Greek dialect of Aeolic. King George of Greece was so impressed that he awarded Robertson both a laurel and an olive branch.

Despite de Coubertin's hope that the Olympics would soon be the greatest of all sporting events, it took some decades to achieve this, and the games were at first shunned by established athletics organisations. Alfred Flatow of Germany, who won three gold medals and one silver in gymnastics at the 1896 Olympics, was banned from other international competitions for two years, for 'taking part in an unauthorised event'. The 1900 Olympic Games in Paris included a cross-country run, baseball, 'Irish sports' and 'Bohemian gymnastics', all of which were soon dropped. The third games were held in St Louis, Missouri, in 1904. Despite lasting for four and a half months, and staging the Olympic debuts of boxing, dumbbells and the decathlon, they were overshadowed by the St Louis World's Fair, marking the centenary of the Louisiana Purchase.

By 1906, despite his huge efforts to rouse the interest of sportsmen around the world, there was a danger that de Coubertin's great idea would fizzle out and disappear. But twice in the twentieth century London showed its mettle by coming to the rescue of the Olympic Games and putting them on only two years from the start of planning.

Olympics organisers have sold advertising space in their programmes since the 1920s.

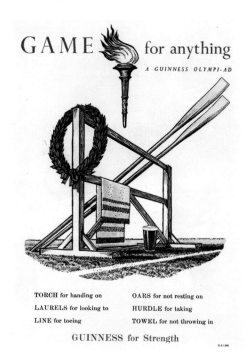

GAME for anything

*A GUINNESS OLYMPI-AD*

TORCH for handing on  
LAURELS for looking to  
LINE for toeing  

OARS for not resting on  
HURDLE for taking  
TOWEL for not throwing in  

GUINNESS for Strength

# THE DRILL THAT MAKES WOMAN PHYSICALLY PERFECT.

## DANISH DIANAS: THE SENSATION OF THE OLYMPIC GAMES.

At the Olympic Games the most beautiful exhibition of gymnastics was given by the team of Danish girl athletes, who among all the competitors in the Stadium were unsurpassed for splendid physical development and grace of movement. The prettiness of their "ensemble" was increased by their charming costume, which was of cream colour with amber stockings.

# THE FIRST LONDON OLYMPICS: 1908

THE FOURTH OLYMPIC GAMES were due to be staged in Rome in 1908, but when Mount Vesuvius erupted in 1906 Italy needed all its resources to rebuild Naples. London stepped in to hold the games, with only two years to prepare.

The Franco-British Exhibition was about to be held at Shepherd's Bush in west London. The White City, as the site soon came to be known, was a huge complex of gleaming white shopping malls, palaces of arts, boating lakes and amusements, including the giant electrically powered 'Flip-Flap'. The organisers agreed to expand the site to include a sports arena big enough to hold 68,000 seats and standing room for 23,000 people. It had a cycling track around the outside of the running track, a football pitch in the middle, and platforms for gymnastics and wrestling. Beside this was a 100-metre swimming pool with a high-diving board. It was built in only ten months at a cost of £85,000 – roughly equivalent to £5 million today.

This was the first Olympics with an opening ceremony. Over two thousand male athletes from twenty-two nations paraded round the stadium with their national flags, in front of crowned royalty, the International Olympic Committee (IOC) and anyone who could afford tickets at one guinea each.

Flags can create all sorts of problems. Finland was then part of the Russian Empire, but the Finnish athletes refused to march behind the Russian flag, so they marched on their own with no flag. The Swedish flag had accidentally been left out of the display above the stadium, so the Swedish team did not parade at all.

Relations between Britain and the United States were already strained but the situation was made worse when the American flag was accidentally flown at half-mast. The American flag-bearer, the shot-putter Ralph Rose, failed to dip his flag as he passed in front of King Edward VII. When asked about his apparent disrespect, he said in defiance, 'The US flag dips to no earthly king.' Since then the American flag has never been lowered to a monarch.

The United States team was already annoyed that Britain had set the rules, and that all the officials were British. The head of the American team,

**FRANCO-BRITS.**
AN INTERCHANGE OF COMPLIMENTS

THE ARRIVAL OF PRESIDENT FALLIERES.
(UNPRECEDENTED? — BUT, IN THESE DAYS OF INNOVATIONS, WHY NOT? C'EST UNE IDÉE MAGNIFIQUE.)

Above, left: Willie Grenfell, Lord Desborough of Taplow, chairman of the British Olympic Council. The perfect Edwardian gentleman sportsman, he played cricket, fenced, sculled the English Channel, shot bears, hunted foxes, climbed the Matterhorn and swam the Niagara Falls in a snowstorm.

Above, right: The 'Flip-Flap' gave Edwardians a view of the White City stadium from 150 feet up.

Left: People were hopeful that the Olympics would bring the French and British closer. President Fallières and King Edward VII talk amicably. 'Unprecedented?' asks *The Bystander*, 'but in these days of innovations, why not? C'est une idée magnifique.'

Opposite, top: Cigarette card showing the shot-putter Ralph Rose, who failed to lower the United States flag to the King.

Opposite, bottom: The twenty-two national teams march into White City on a damp July day for the opening ceremony.

James Sullivan, was also the president of the Amateur Athletic Union of America. He believed passionately that sport would improve life for poor young men. He was also convinced that the Olympic rules favoured the British team. His team lodged official protests at every opportunity. Their pole-vaulters, for example, expected to land on sawdust and sand, not the hard ground. To Britons, the Americans' determination to win was brash and unsportsmanlike, and their fans' habit of rooting for their own side was considered ungentlemanly.

## TUG-OF-WAR

The first major controversy was in the tug-of-war, a sport not well-known in the United States. The rules prohibited the wearing of footwear with projecting nails or tips, so the American team wore ordinary shoes. They had little understanding of the fine art of tug-of-war, and at the call of 'Heave' the team of eight sturdy Liverpool policemen pulled them over like a line of schoolboys. The crowd erupted into laughter. Immediately James Sullivan protested that the Liverpudlians' heavy boots gave them an unfair

PUTTING THE WEIGHT.

The City of London Police team, who won gold for the tug-of-war, with their coaches.

Spalding's Athletic Library, edited by James Sullivan, gave readers in the United States all the Olympic results, for only 10 cents.

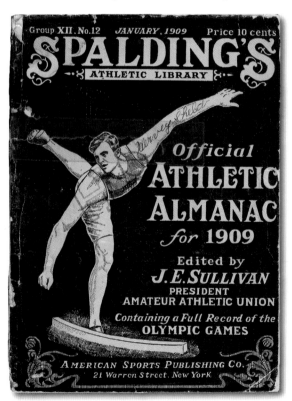

advantage, but it was pointed out that they were simply wearing ordinary police boots. The Liverpool team offered the second pull (of the best of three) in their socks, but the American team were convinced that the British had cheated and they stormed off. Their complaint was dismissed and in protest the American team withdrew. This left three British teams: the City of London Police won gold, Liverpool got silver and the Metropolitan Police bronze.

The Olympic Games were organised as a private enterprise, with no government assistance. But weekday sport then was only for those who could afford to take time off from work, or not work at all, and anyway few people had heard of the Olympics. Also, in the first week it poured with rain and not many people came. The British Olympic Council was so worried that they cancelled many of the planned parties and sightseeing excursions and appealed for donations from the public.

## THE 400-METRES RACE

In the second week, with reduced ticket prices and better weather, over sixty thousand people were packed into the stadium. The 400-metres race, the longest of the sprints, was one lap round the track, without designated lanes or tapes. In the final, the four runners were Lieutenant Wyndham Halswelle from Scotland and three Americans: John Carpenter, William Robbins, and John Taylor, the favourite. Halswelle and Carpenter were neck and neck when Carpenter cut across the track, preventing Halswelle from overtaking. The organisers, aware that this race could be controversial, had placed extra officials – all British – around the track. Without lanes or strings, it was impossible to say whether he broke the rules, but it was considered by the crowd to be unsportsmanlike. They booed their fury and, after much argument with the Americans, the British officials signalled a foul. They declared the race void and Carpenter was disqualified for blocking and elbowing. Sullivan was enraged and felt it was a conspiracy against the Americans. He told his men not to rerun the race two days later. So Halswelle entered the 400-metres final on his own. Running as fast as he could against himself, he won the gold medal.

King Edward VII opened the 1908 Games.

Baron de Coubertin was mystified – he thought that the Olympics would unite nations, not cause further friction: 'I just could not understand Sullivan's attitude here; he shared his team's frenzy and did nothing to calm them down.' Despite the Americans' belief that they were unfairly treated, they still won over half of the track and field events, and set three world records.

The weather was appalling during the first week of the 1908 games.

A few days later, John Taylor was in the winning medley relay team and became the first African-American to win an Olympic gold medal. Sadly, that same year he died of typhoid, aged twenty-five. Halswelle never ran again; he was killed in the First World War in 1915.

Ireland was still part of Great Britain but many Irish athletes felt that they should compete in their own right. Fearing an Irish boycott, the team's name was changed to Great Britain/Ireland, though Ireland competed separately in hockey and polo and won silver medals in both. Irish-American athletes won nearly half of the United States Olympic team's total of twenty-three gold medals.

## SWIMMING

Swimming in the 100-metre pool was of such a high standard that five world records were set. Three of the gold medals were won by Henry Taylor, the son of a Lancashire coal-miner, who had learned to swim in his local canal. He had already won a gold medal in 1906, swimming for a mile in the rough open sea, using the 'trudgen', a double overarm stroke that pre-dated the crawl. He went on to win the famous 13-mile Morecambe Bay race eight times.

Diving was added for the first time, thrilling the spectators as ladies clad in woollen costumes demonstrated springboard diving from a great height. Only weeks before, the pool had been used for the national fly and bait casting championship.

Below: Sybil 'Queenie' Newall was an all-round sportswoman.

Below, right: Many new Olympic sports were added to the list. *The Bystander* magazine wondered if this would include ladies' hopscotch.

## ARCHERY

In 1904 at St Louis women were given their own archery events, which by 1908 drew thirty-six entries. The winner was Sybil 'Queenie' Newall from Britain, who was fifty-three; she remains the oldest woman ever to win Olympic gold. The runner-up was Charlotte Dodd, an exceptional athlete who had won the Wimbledon ladies' tennis singles on five occasions and the British ladies' golf crown, and represented England at hockey, and also excelled at skating and tobogganing. Charlotte and her brother Willie Dodd were

OLYMPIC HOPSCOTCH. MISS 'TILDA BRAHN IS PREPARED TO MEET ALL COMERS ON THE PAVEMENT BY THE RAILINGS OF LINCOLNS INN FIELDS.

descendants of the commander of the British archers at the battle of Agincourt, and were the first brother and sister to win medals. Willie won a gold medal on his forty-first birthday in archery – one of the many older champions in 1908. Henry Blackstaffe won the single sculls at forty; and the tennis player George Hillyard was forty-four years old when he won gold in the men's doubles. Oldest of all was Oscar Swahn of Sweden, who won two rifle-shooting events at sixty years of age. In 1912 and again in 1920, aged seventy-two, he won more medals; he remains the oldest Olympic sportsman to win gold.

Some of the 1908 sports no longer exist. In the standing long jump competitors leant forward as far as they could go without falling over, and then leapt forward. Ray Ewry of the United States won both this and the standing high jump, bringing him a total of ten gold medals over three Olympics. He was known as the 'Human Frog', despite having had polio as a child.

## THE MARATHON

The highlight of the 1908 Olympics for everyone was the marathon, with its dramatic ending. After a week of heavy rain, the day of the marathon was exceptionally hot. Mary, Princess of Wales, started the race from a gilt chair placed outside Windsor Castle, watched by two future kings – Prince Albert and Prince Edward. Over fifty men set off, followed by their coaches on bicycles. They all wore the regulation short-sleeved jersey and loose cotton drawers but chose their own footwear. The Americans had soaked their socks in tallow wax, while the Canadians bathed their feet in whisky and alum. Other contestants had taken advantage of the free samples of Antiseptic Military Foot Powder.

They were led by the favourite, Tom Longboat, a Canadian Iroquois who had only just qualified as an amateur. His manager, Tom Flanagan, was certainly in it for the money: he made bets, sold tickets and encouraged commercial sponsorship – while paying Longboat nothing but his living

The start of the marathon at Windsor, attended by the Princess of Wales.

TOM LONGBOAT

Tom Longboat
of Canada was
the favourite for
the marathon.

Map of the 1908
marathon route
from Windsor
Castle to White
City.

expenses. Longboat enjoyed life as a celebrity and he was not pleased when Flanagan took him to rural Ireland to train. Sullivan, realising that Canada might win the marathon, objected but was overruled. Flanagan was delighted – if his protégé won the marathon, he could go professional and they would both get rich.

The men slogged on through Slough, and the British runners, Jack Price and Tom Lord, 'a wiry coal-miner, half-greyhound, half-bulldog', led the way as they ran down Uxbridge High Street. Oxo sponsored the marathon and had set up booths promoting their health-sustaining beefy drink, served hot or cold. They also offered raisins, rice pudding and eau-de-Cologne. On the men ran, through Harrow, Willesden, Harlesden and across Wormwood Scrubs. Over a quarter of a million people lined the streets – the biggest sporting event in history.

The official marathon distance had been 26 miles, but in 1908 an extra 385 yards round the track was added so that the finish was in front of the royal box. It has remained that length ever since. Longboat, known as the 'Indian Wonder', collapsed in a heap after being giving champagne to restore him. Some people suspected he had also been given strychnine, then covertly used by long-distance runners.

Drugs were banned, but 'stimulants' such as calves' foot jelly, tea mixed with raw eggs, and champagne were allowed. With no thought of dehydration, the runners all soon weakened in the heat. One by one they dropped out, and Dorando Pietri, a diminutive twenty-two-year-old Italian

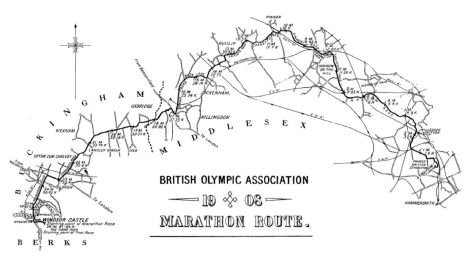

BRITISH OLYMPIC ASSOCIATION
19 ✧ 08
MARATHON ROUTE.

pastry baker, crept up to the lead. Pietri was a slight young man with a shock of curly black hair and a dapper moustache. Self-trained, his running style was all over the place, his breath coming in 'great heaves'. His coach, beside him on a bicycle, waved madly at him, as Irish-American Johnny Hayes, also twenty-two years old, came up hot on his heels. Only four Britons were now running.

At White City the capacity crowd cheered as Pietri staggered into the stadium – 'a tired man, dazed, bewildered, hardly conscious, in red shorts and white vest, his hair white with dust,' reported *The Times*. 'He looks about him, hardly knowing where he is. Just the knowledge that somehow, by some desperate resolve of determination, he must get round the 300 yards to the tape of the finish.' The crowd gasped in horror as he set off in the wrong direction around the track and then collapsed.

Johnny Hayes in his United States Olympic uniform, on a cigarette card.

'He was within a few yards of my seat,' wrote Arthur Conan Doyle, author of the Sherlock Holmes stories. 'Amid stooping figures and grasping hands I caught a glimpse of the haggard, yellow face, the glazed, expressionless eyes, the lank, black hair streaked across the brow. Surely he is done now. He cannot rise again.'

Johnny Hayes entered the stadium and caught up with the staggering Pietri, who fell five times. Spurred on by the cheering crowd, the Clerk of the Course and the medical attendant helped him over the finish line. Pietri was declared

Dorando Pietri breaks the tape as he is helped over the finish line of the marathon.

the winner. Of course the United States officials quickly filed a complaint; and after some hours Pietri was disqualified and Hayes was awarded the gold medal. He was carried round the track on a table by his team-mates, two of whom had won the silver and bronze medals – ignored by the crowd, who felt Pietri was the true winner, having so valiantly tried to win. If only the officials had not helped him, he might have done so. Pietri was taken off to hospital, delirious, on a stretcher, and, as rumours that he had died circulated, Anglo-American relations reached their lowest point for over a hundred years.

Later that night Baron de Coubertin reminded his friends that, only a few days before, the Bishop of Pennsylvania had preached a sermon in St Paul's Cathedral in honour of the athletes. He had said: 'The important thing in Olympics is not so much winning as taking part. The essential thing in life is not conquering but fighting well.'

Pietri's story mirrored the legend of the original marathon, when the Greek messenger Pheidippides died after running all day with the news of the Greek victory at the Battle of Marathon in 490 BC.

At the closing ceremony, when all the prizes and medals were handed out, the Americans' fury increased when Pietri received even bigger cheers than the gold medallist, and Queen Alexandra presented him with a special gold cup.

Pietri exhibited the cup at the Hammersmith Palace of Varieties, and Irving Berlin composed a song called 'Dorando'. Johnny Hayes was fêted only by the President of the United States: 'I am so glad that a New York boy won it,'

Above: The winner of the marathon, Johnny Hayes, is carried round the stadium on a table.

Left: Postcard showing Dorando Pietri with the cup specially awarded to him.

Theodore Roosevelt told him. Pietri and Hayes both became professional runners, sometimes competing against each other in exhibition races.

After the closing firework display, attended by Edward VII and President Fallières of France, police had to quell a riot incited by young men carrying 'Votes for women' placards.

The Winter Olympics in 1908 took place in the autumn and included football, rugby, lacrosse and hockey. Figure skating was included for the first time, taking place at the smart Prince's Skating Rink, in Knightsbridge. Madge Syers, the daughter of a British hosiery merchant, won two medals and set the fashion for wearing shorter skirts in bright colours. Already an international champion, she skated 'with her own particular dash and finish', according to *The Times*.

Some Olympic sports have had a very short life. Motorboat racing took place in a gale in the Solent off Southampton. In each of the three events, only two boats started and one boat made it round the course of 40 nautical miles. The winner of the 'Under 60 feet' class, *Gyrinus*, a long narrow boat with an extra crewman to bail water, was designed by Sir John Thornycroft, who also designed and built the world's first torpedo boats. After 1908, motorboat racing was cancelled as an Olympic sport.

The total cost of arranging the games was £15,000 (worth £850,000 today), of which over one-third was spent on 'entertainments'. Only a quarter of the income of £21,377 was from ticket sales; the rest was from donations, leaving a profit of £6,377.

Despite all the political problems, the first London Olympics were a great success and paved the way for advances in judging, officiating and scoring for future Olympic Games. London took the Olympics from sideshow status to being a world sports event. If the 1908 Games had not been so well organised and brought in such crowds, the Olympic Games might well have fizzled out and be remembered now only by sports historians.

There was a break for the First World War, but after it the Olympic Games continued to grow in size and importance. At the 1936 games in Berlin, Hitler used the Olympics to impress the world with the strength and efficiency of Nazi Germany.

Tokyo was selected to host the 1940 Olympics but when the Japanese army invaded Manchuria in 1938 the 1940 games were reallocated to Helsinki. However, the Second World War intervened and there were no Olympics in either 1940 or 1944.

Ray Ewry of the United States was known as the 'Human Frog' for winning both the standing long jump and the standing high jump.

RAY C. EWRY

# MAKE DO AND
# MEND: 1948

In 1944 the IOC started to plan the fourteenth Olympiad for 1948. They knew that no nation could afford to send its athletes overseas, and that, despite the Blitz, London would be the only city in Europe with enough resources. So London was chosen, even before the war had ended. With this second opportunity to host the games, London had to prove to the world that it could succeed, and that the Olympics were about sport and not politics.

After the Nazi-dominated games in Berlin twelve years earlier, it was important to reinstate the Olympic ideals of equality and fair play, without political or racial propaganda. The founder of the modern Olympics, Baron Pierre de Coubertin, believed that sport would lead to world peace. But although the Second World War had ended, various conflicts rumbled on. There was a civil war in Greece, and Arabs and Jews were bombing each other in Israel. The 'Iron Curtain' divided Europe, with most of eastern Europe falling under the domination of the USSR. The phrase 'Cold War' was coined; and the Soviet Union had blockaded Berlin, preventing Britain from getting food or other supplies in by road. Hosting the 1948 Olympics would be a tough challenge for any city, even London.

The idea of holding the Olympics in London was not popular with the British public, the press or the government. Unemployment was high; food, clothing and petrol were still rationed; bombed buildings had not been rebuilt and housing was in very short supply.

Just as in 1908, the British Olympic Committee (BOC) had less than two years to set up the Games. As in 1908, the members were all men with titles or high military rank, which gave them the advantage of access to people in high places.

The Second World War had left Britain almost bankrupt. So the Olympic organisers had to 'make do and mend'. They planned the games as if it were a military operation, on a tiny budget. They decided that competitors would get bed linen but should bring their own towels and soap. They invited each country to bring its own gymnastic equipment. When swimming officials asked for their Claridge's Hotel bill to be paid after a meeting in London, the

Opposite: John Mark arrives in the Empire Stadium, Wembley, with the Olympic flame in 1948. The quote on the scoreboard was not de Coubertin's. The Bishop of Pennsylvania said it in 1908.

treasurer, Harold Abrahams, fumed: 'All the staff is working on an austerity basis and with the utmost economy, so equal care must be exercised by us all.' When Mr Beardsall of the Olympic postal department asked to be compensated for a pair of trousers that had been damaged by a nail, he was given the money only after he forfeited the entire suit.

Many people offered to help. Billy Butlin, the owner of six holiday camps, invited the British athletics team to train for a week at Clacton-on-Sea. During the war the camp had housed prisoners of war and now it had reopened with an amusement park, private beach and L-shaped swimming pool. The contestants were greeted by Gladys Painter, the first-ever 'Redcoat'.

Coca-Cola, Nescafé, Craven A cigarettes, Gillette razors, Martel brandy, Sloan's liniment and Brylcreem all provided corporate sponsorship by buying advertising space in the official programmes. Programmes and souvenirs had to be approved, and permission to use the Olympic logo of five connected rings cost £250.

By 1948 there were over seventy nations that had Olympic committees, but Germany and Japan were not invited, following the precedent set after 1918. The German IOC member, Dr Karl von Halt, claimed that as he lived

Lucky members of the British team in 1948 stayed at Butlin's holiday camp at Clacton-on-Sea under the eye of Captain Bond, the camp trainer.

**BUTLIN'S HOLIDAY CAMP**
**CLACTON-ON-SEA**
IT'S QUICKER BY RAIL

THE ROUTE
OF THE
OLYMPIC TORCH
RELAY

The torch relay originated with the 1936 Olympics. In 1948 the torch travelled 1,975 miles through eight countries and over two seas.

in British-occupied Berlin he could come as a Briton. He was firmly told that visas were not available. Then the Japanese announced their intention to send a team. As the peace agreement had not yet been signed, Japan was still technically Britain's enemy. The Japanese were reminded that under the rules of the occupation none of their subjects could leave the country.

Since 1936 borders, affiliations and even national identities had changed. When Finland competed in 1908, it was a province of Russia, but it had been independent since 1920. Lithuania, Estonia and Latvia all won medals at the Olympics between 1920 and 1936, but in 1940 they became part of the Soviet Union. Since the revolution of 1917, the Soviets had considered the Olympic Games an aspect of Western imperialism. The USSR had received every encouragement to set up an Olympic committee but after the Berlin blockade British attitudes became considerably chillier. So the Soviet embassy bought tickets for every event and reported back to Stalin that the Olympic Games were an ideal way to demonstrate the supremacy of communism to the capitalist world.

Italy was invited on the strength of having joined the Allies late in the war. India and Pakistan, divided in 1947, were represented separately for the first

Bernard Bullen, one of the 1,688 men who carried the specially designed aluminium Olympic torch for two miles.

time. The Palestinian team was already in training when it was told that its registration had been withdrawn because of the creation of Israel. The IOC then averted an Arab boycott by ruling that Israel could not compete until it had an Olympic committee.

Over fifty teams came, from all over the world. The New Zealand team spent five weeks at sea on a small cargo ship and arrived thoroughly seasick and unfit, despite daily races round the deck. Most of the United States team travelled on SS *America*. 'I shook hands with my first black American on board ship,' remembered rifle-shooter Arthur Jackson. Ramadan ended during the games, though no officials realised that Muslims had to compete while fasting. Probably never before in London had so many creeds, classes and races come together as equals.

It was both a happy and a sad meeting of nations. All the European teams had lost athletes in the war. Jewish Hungarian fencers and Dutch gymnasts who had taken part in the 1936 Olympics had perished in Nazi concentration camps. Many North American athletes had died fighting in the Pacific or Europe. The British team had lived through the Blitz, many had fought in North Africa, France and Italy, and all were acutely conscious of friends and rivals who had perished in the war.

## ARENAS

There was neither the time nor the money to build a new Olympic stadium, nor any sports arenas. So they had to use arenas that had survived the Blitz. At the Empire Pool (now Wembley Arena) the ice-skating rink was removed, the black-out paint scraped off the ceiling and the pool renovated. After a week of swimming and diving, a boxing ring was constructed over the pool on a bridge built from steel girders hired from Sheffield. The weeds and the wartime barrage balloons were removed from Herne Hill cycling velodrome in south London. The Marine Spa

Left: The British team waiting outside for the opening ceremony. 'We looked like French onion sellers,' said oarsman Tony Butcher, who took this photograph.

in Torquay was repainted to serve as the Olympic headquarters for sailing. Finland donated timber to replace the rotting floor at Harringay Arena, to be used for basketball. The King lent Windsor Great Park for the cycle road race.

At the Empire Stadium, Wembley, the greyhound track was replaced with cinders from the hearths of Leicester. The changing rooms were spruced up with showers and 'plunge baths', and signs reading 'Toilets' were repainted to 'Ladies' and 'Gentlemen'. German prisoners of war pushed wheelbarrows and operated pneumatic drills to create a new road called Olympic Way, leading from Wembley Park station. The road is still there.

On 29 July eighty thousand people gathered for the opening ceremony at Wembley. 'The scene, with most men in their shirt sleeves and the women in flimsy summer frocks,' reported the *Wembley News*, 'reminded one more of an American sports arena than the usual prosaic British assembly.' It was the hottest day since 1911. Men shaded their heads with folded newspapers and knotted handkerchiefs; the women rolled down their seamed stockings and raised their umbrellas as parasols. A student called Roger Bannister, who had been helping the organisers, proved his worth as a runner when the British team realised they had no Union Flag. He sprinted back to the car park, grabbed a flag and pole from his boss's car and ran back to the team just as they were about to march into the stadium.

The seven thousand pigeons released at the opening ceremony arrived by train that morning and were kept well supplied with water in the stadium.

John Glenister was a fifteen-year-old Boy Scout from Harrow. 'Being already 6 foot tall, I was picked to mark the saluting base, by the Royal Box. We had to stand there for ages before the ceremony began, so I sat down. The Scout next to me fainted. As the athletes marched past my flag, they did an "eyes right" to acknowledge King George VI. It felt as if they were all looking at me!'

Even though southern Ireland had gained its independence, the Irish still had problems. Their manager insisted his team was called 'Ireland', not 'Eire', and they wanted to march between Iraq and Italy, and not between Egypt and Finland. He failed to win that round but kept up the pressure on the rights of athletes born in Ireland to compete for whichever nation they chose.

Malta's team consisted of one single athlete, a sprinter called Nestor Jacono, who remembered: 'The people roared their greetings for "Brave Little Malta" with deafening cheers for our team from the George Cross island, marching in a sea of space

between Luxembourg and Mexico.' Jacono came last in the first heat of the shortest race – the 100-metres dash.

As the host, Great Britain was the last team to enter the stadium. Peter Elliot was a young diver from London, who marched in beside the 6-foot 4-inch tall wrestler Kenneth Richmond, later famous for banging the huge gong at the start of J. Arthur Rank films. 'They called out "Great Britain" and I looked up. There were tears running down Ken's cheeks. There was this amazing roar, like seven hundred lions, and I started crying too. I realised how amazing it all was. Ken and I wept our way round the stadium. I was looking for my parents and I couldn't see them and this giant beside me was sobbing his heart out. It was the emotion after the war, the emotion of any Olympics, it is a competition against the world, you represent your whole nation.'

The King opened the games, a fanfare of trumpets played and seven thousand pigeons were released into the sky. 'The flash of wings was like a snowstorm on that brilliant summer afternoon and as the pigeons swooshed round, seven thousand shadows on the grass added to the thrill of the moment,' declared the *Wembley News.*

Over fifty national teams marched into the Empire Stadium, Wembley, to the sound of the Guards Band and eighty-thousand spectators on the opening day of the fourteenth Olympic Games.

## HOUSING

There was no special Olympic Village. The four thousand competitors, their coaches and team managers were accommodated all round London in RAF camps, schools and colleges. One legacy of the war was the Ministry of Supply, which overnight converted classrooms into hostels. These 'housing centres' were then equipped by the Ministry of Works with beds, rush mats and 'utility' cupboards.

'Comfort but few luxuries,' reported the *Surrey Comet* of the Richmond Park site. 'Every effort has been made to provide a pleasant "home from home" while ingenuity has been shown in economy and reuse of materials. Army quarters have been converted into shops, a laundry, and a bank.

Spectators keep their gaze on the field while a boy checks a programme of the many events on offer.

Each dormitory has linoleum and sprung iron beds with horse hair mattresses and coloured quilts. It looks comfortable and yet bears the stamp of austerity. No charges could be levelled against money being spent on exorbitant luxury.'

At Wembley County School the art room was furnished with easy chairs, a radio and a piano, and the dining room with 'folk-weave curtains', tablecloths, flowers and coloured mats. There were no telephones for competitors, so schoolboys who owned bicycles were taken on as messengers. 'We received no pay,' remembered Dennis Newton, then fifteen, 'but we got three decent meals a day, and were taken by bus to the opening and closing ceremonies at Wembley.'

Horlicks was provided free to all athletes at the housing centres. 'Horlicks helps you to get the right kind of deep, refreshing sleep,' claimed the manufacturers.

'There were no parties at RAF Uxbridge,' recalled British sprinter Alastair McCorquadale, 'just training and early to bed. No alcohol was available; only gallons of Horlicks malted milk.'

The sexes were strictly segregated, and the women stayed in three colleges. 'The Domestic Science College behind Victoria station was dark and cramped,' Ngaire Lane, the only woman from New Zealand, remembered. 'But there was always lively company. Micheline Ostermeyer,

All conveniences were provided at the Olympic housing centres.

the French discus thrower, entertained us on the piano. We went to Wembley in a double-decker bus, everyone on board singing their national songs.'

Spectators who could not afford hotels could pay 5s a night to sleep in marquees with rows of camp beds, set up in Northwick Park near Harrow.

## FOOD

With food rationing still in place, British athletes had to train on 2,600 calories per day, which included one slice of bacon, one ounce of cheese and one egg a week. This was increased to a docker's rations of 3,900 calories only when they were selected for the Olympic team. For some, this was only days before the games started. A few British athletes received food parcels from Canada and Australia, which contained tinned fruit and chocolate powder. 'Eat plenty of cooked beetroot,' advised Britain's swimming coach, Harry Koskie, 'and at least one halibut oil capsule per day.'

Footballer Angus Carmichael found his Olympic blazer got him extra food. 'It was quite embarrassing, with food rationing on for everybody else. Restaurants would pile up your plate with extra food, saying "Eat up, we need to build up the British team".'

Commercial restaurants catered at the housing centres, chosen according to the nationality of the resident athletes. Veeraswamy's Indian restaurant in Swallow Street in Piccadilly cooked for the hundred Indians and Burmese at

*Above: Harrison Dillard, McDonald Bailey, Alastair McCorquadale, Lloyd Labeach, Barney Ewell and Mel Patton in the final of the 100-metres dash, the first time that 'photo-finish' technology was used. Dillard won in 10.3 seconds, Ewell got silver, and Labeach, the sole member of the Panama team, took bronze.*

*Right: Maurice Graham, aged sixteen from Yorkshire, stood on a wall overlooking Olympic Way and took this photograph with his Box Brownie camera.*

27

'Drugs! We had drugs in 1948,' said hurdler Joe Birrell: 'We ate Horlicks tablets by the handful!'

A firm in Dunstable bought up the cuttings of films and sold them as single frames to be seen through a 'Vuefinder'.

Pinner County School; and Ley On's Chop Suey from Soho fed the Chinese team at Kilburn Technical School.

Visiting teams were encouraged to bring food to share with others. Denmark sent 160,000 eggs. China sent oiled bamboo shoots, dried shrimps and green tea. Hungary sent poppy seeds, paprika and twenty thousand lemons. Ceylon (Sri Lanka) brought coconuts and spices. Dutch farmers sent vegetables, ginger cakes and cheese. Mexico sent liver, kidneys and tripe; and the New Zealand team brought with them condensed milk and mutton dripping.

The Americans were very popular with their fifteen thousand bars of chocolate, five thousand steaks and daily flights from Los Angeles of enriched white flour and fresh fruit. The French team sent one railway wagon filled with *Premier Cru classé* Mouton-Rothschild wine, and another with vegetables and 1,700 kg of steak.

Dr Magnus Pyke, the chief government nutritionist, studied the visitors' 'peculiar dietary habits'. Each day he took away samples of their food in Kilner jars to assess their calorific value. This was the first scientific study of sports nutrition. He discovered that the Australians had two boiled eggs and a chop each for breakfast, and the Mexicans ate six thousand calories a day each of chillis, tripe and beans but not many vegetables.

## UNIFORM

The British team were each issued with a black blazer, tie and white trousers. 'The Olympic tie was so short it stopped half way down your chest,' laughed oarsman Bert Bushnell.

Footballers were given shirts and baggy shorts but provided their own boots. The English Football Association lent them second-hand tracksuits, which had to be handed back after the games. A free pair of Cooper's white Y-front pants was handed out to every male British competitor. Sales of the new-fangled underwear soared when foreign competitors saw them in the dressing rooms.

The British women had to make or borrow their own sports kits, but they were each given a navy-blue serge blazer and a white cotton frock. 'We had to buy our own shoes, which were expensive, and our own socks, which used up two ration coupons,' said the high-jumper Dorothy Tyler. 'My Olympic uniform was the smartest thing I owned,' said the long-jumper Lorna Lee-Price; 'I even wore it to my sister's wedding.'

## TRANSPORT

Petrol was strictly rationed, so, to get from the housing centres to the various venues, competitors were given free passes for the recently nationalised London Transport buses and Underground. After the cyclists complained

Above left: Lorna Lee-Price, a seventeen-year-old long-jumper from Kent, in her Olympic uniform – 'the smartest clothes owned'.

Above: This rowing vest was worn by Bobby Collins in the coxed four at Henley-on-Thames. 'When we were issued with white sleeveless singlets, we felt very naked.'

E. McDONALD BAILEY
(GREAT BRITAIN)
*Native of Trinidad and the finest sprint runner outside the U.S.*
50 OLYMPICS 1948 N? 3

J. RYAN
(GREAT BRITAIN)
*Best known of all British amateur boxers and a strong fancy for the welterweight title.*
50 OLYMPICS 1948 N? 14

Above: Turf cigarette cards: McDonald Bailey of Trinidad was a popular sprinter in the 100-metres dash final. 'My greatest achievement was coming sixth in the 1948 Olympics,' he said.

that the roads had too many potholes, they were ferried to their races in an old bus with half the seats removed.

At first the British press considered the Olympics a waste of public money, but soon over two thousand journalists from all over the world had gathered. Female divers in the Empire Pool provided a popular opportunity to photograph scantily clad competitors, while on the wireless live coverage of the games shared the BBC Home Service with *Music While You Work*, *Children's Hour* and *Gert and Daisy's Working Party*.

## THE 10,000-METRES RACE

Just as in 1908, the team from the United States reckoned they were the best. They were right – there were more of them, they had proper coaches and they had not suffered food rationing for eight years.

When the 10,000-metres final started at 6 p.m. it was still a scorching day. Even so, athletes were advised not to drink. Harold Nelson had come all the way from New Zealand and had carried the flag the day before. 'I was thirsty but didn't drink. We had been advised not to drink for the day before a race. A dessert-spoon of honey got rid of all the liquid in the stomach.'

Few people noticed a wiry man called Emil Zatopek as the field of thirty-one runners set off. Representing Czechoslovakia, Zatopek was an army officer aged twenty-six. He had invented 'interval training' by running and walking for miles in his army boots. It was said he even carried his wife, an Olympic javelin-thrower, on his back. Zatopek began slowly and then proceeded to lap his thirty opponents. At 5 feet 8 inches tall, with a large balding head, he did not look like a runner. 'When Zatopek ran, he grimaced, pumping his arms, with his tongue hanging out,' said fellow-runner Alain Mimoun-o-Kacha, a French-Algerian. 'He worked like a woodcutter in the forest. But he didn't cut down trees, he cut down other runners.'

Emil Zatopek of Czechoslovakia set a new Olympic record when he ran 10,000 metres in 29 minutes 59.6 seconds.

The crowd was thrilled at the sight of him, his head nodding from side to side, and shouted, 'Za-to-pek, Za-to-pek, Za-to-pek'. The chant could be heard all round Wembley. He ran fast for 400 metres, then slowed for 100 metres, then surged ahead again. This left the other runners totally confused, for each time he slowed they thought he was finished, and just as they caught

There was no barrier between the track and spectators. The summer holidays had begun and on the first day children sat on the low wall in the baking heat.

When it rained, Danish runner H. E. Christensen watched the 800-metres final from a stretcher after breaking his leg in the second heat.

Above: Twenty-year-old Paul Elvstrom of Denmark asks advice of Air Commodore Arthur McDonald, aged forty-five, of Britain, before they begin their six Firefly dinghy races in Torbay, Devon. McDonald won silver and Elvstrom the gold; he competed in seven subsequent Olympic Games.

Above right: Bantamweight Joe de Pietro of the United States won gold in the two hands clean and press event by lifting 105 kg, breaking the Olympic record. He was only 4 feet 8 inches tall.

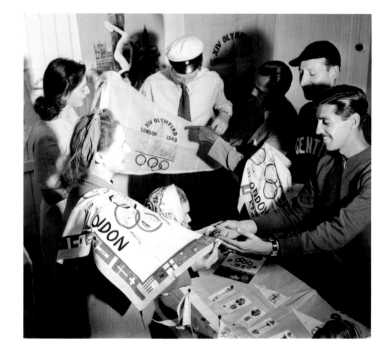

Right: Argentinian athletes buying souvenirs.

up with him he would break forward, or start chatting to them. Over the final 4,000 metres he lapped every other runner. Zatopek won, knocking nearly twelve seconds off the Olympic record. Mimoun came in second, and the two men hugged each other in delight. A few days later Zatopek won silver in the 5,000 metres.

'After all those dark days of the war,' he said, 'the bombing, the killing and the starvation, the revival of the Olympics was as if the sun had come out.'

## SPORTSWOMEN

Women in 1948 made up only 10 per cent of the competitors and were allowed to compete in only nine athletics events, which included the long jump, shot putting and short races. They were still considered too feeble for much more effort, in case it brought on early senility or confused their internal organs.

At the European Athletic Championships in 1946 two of the fastest women were afterwards discovered to be men, so in 1948 sex testing was introduced. Much to everyone's embarrassment, this involved a doctor peering into the underwear of female competitors to check for 'sexual abnormalities'.

Even so, it was a woman who was the star of the London Olympics. Fanny Blankers-Koen was born in the Netherlands in 1918 and made her Olympic début as a high-jumper in 1936 in Berlin. Her coach was her husband, the Olympic triple jumper Jan Blankers, and in 1940 they married

HENLEY ON THAMES
*Souvenir Guide on the occasion of the*
OLYMPIC REGATTA 1948

Henley-on-Thames hosted the rowing and canoeing – but could not afford the £250 copyright fee for the Olympic rings symbol on their programme.

Fanny Blankers-Koen and Maureen Gardner in the 80-metres hurdles final.

The British women's swimming team: an opportunity to view attractive young bodies.

and had a son. She then broke world records in the 100 metres, high jump and long jump. After the birth of her daughter five years later, she trained with her children playing beside her. She was now a world-record holder in six events and was nicknamed the 'Flying Housewife'. The British press said that as a thirty-year-old mother of two she was far too old. The *Daily Graphic* revealed: 'She is an expert cook and darns socks with artistry. Her greatest love next to racing is housework.'

Women were allowed to enter a maximum of four events each, so she had to choose carefully which ones. Douglas Burns, a former navigator in the RAF, was on an Underground train from Piccadilly Circus. 'Standing next to me, hanging on a strap, was Fanny Blankers-Koen. She told me she would definitely run the 100 metres; it would depend on how the others were programmed for the rest.'

After a bright start to the Olympics, it was now raining, with puddles all over the track, but spirits were not dampened. Phoebe Tyson, aged fifteen, from Hampshire was in the stadium. 'There was a tremendous camaraderie in the crowd: everyone was so glad to be there, proud of the effort that Britain had put into staging the games, and excited to see competitors from other countries. Even when it poured with rain, I never heard a word of complaint. Many of the athletes smiled and spoke to us. My proudest moment came when Fanny Blankers-Koen gave me her cardigan to hold whilst she ran.'

Rowing pairs race upstream towards the finish at Leander Club, Henley-on-Thames.

'Mrs Blankers-Koen, with her orange shorts and her fair floating hair, strode home to victory with all the irresistible surge of the great men sprinters, and stealing half their thunder,' wrote *The Times*.

In only eight days Blankers-Koen won a total of eleven heats and finals, and four gold medals, for the 4 x 100-metres relay, 200-metres dash, 100-metres dash and 80-metres hurdles. Sir Arthur Porritt, 1924 Olympic medallist, royal doctor and medical adviser to the BOC, wrote: 'Apart from her unique physical prowess,

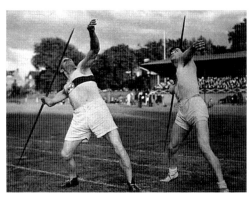

she has a quiet, self-contained but essentially friendly temperament which allows her to face up to the big occasion with an apparent cool equanimity. But anyone who has seen her run one hundred per cent and then a little more, concentration evident on her face in the last few strides of a race, will know the remarkable intensity of the effort that is being so beautifully produced.'

Jock and Malcolm Dalrymple – the only father and son to compete in Olympic javelin throwing.

James Pilditch was a student helper at RAF Uxbridge Olympic housing centre. 'To celebrate Fanny's gold medals, the Dutch students held a dance for her. We all wore our best suits but the nearest that the Dutch students could get to this was their pyjama jackets with their collars turned up.'

When she arrived back in the Netherlands, the customs officer asked if she had any gold to declare. 'Yes,' she confessed, 'four gold medals.' 'They are only silver-gilt,' said the officer, 'but they should be made of diamonds.'

Dorothy Tyler, aged thirty, was Britain's greatest high-jumper. She had won silver in the 1936 Berlin Olympics. While she trained, her husband Richard looked after their sons, Barry and David.

Thousands of people lined the streets of Amsterdam to watch her pass in a horse-drawn carriage. Her neighbours presented her with a bicycle – 'so you don't have to run so much,' they said.

Mary Glen Haig of Great Britain was another thirty-year-old Olympian woman with style. Her father had fenced in the 1900 Olympics and taught her from the age of ten.

'Before I was allowed to hold a foil,' she said. 'I had to get my footwork right and, when I was eventually given one, the professor would conduct controlled bouts. When we went to a competition in France, my brother and I had to sit up all night on the ferry, get a train at the other end and then compete after that.'

During and after the Second World War she worked as a hospital administrator. 'Even after I was chosen for the Olympic team, fencing practice had to fit around the men. My training was walking round the hospital all day. The night before my event I was working until 8 o'clock at King's College Hospital.' Then she stayed at the women's centre in Victoria. 'I had to take my rations with me from the hospital kitchen.'

The fencing took place in the cavernous Palace of Engineering next to Wembley Stadium. Hung with the flags of the sixteen competing nations, it echoed to the clashing steel of attacks and ripostes. With her precision energy, Glen Haig beat the other seven competitors and reached the final.

In 1948 sportsmen and women of all classes, races and creeds could compete freely together, as the French magazine *Point du Vue* shows. 'This photograph provoked a scandal in the United States, where whites and blacks do not fraternise. But in the joy of winning their event, R. B. Cochran and the "chocolate" Harrison Dillard paid no attention to racist doctrine.'

PALACE OF ENGINEERING
WEMBLEY
XIV OLYMPIAD
LONDON
1948
Press Photographer's
Messenger

Left: Women's foil fencing taking place in the Palace of Engineering at Wembley.

Above: A press pass for the fencing. The reverse states: 'This pass is used upon the express understanding that the holder shall not take cinematograph pictures of any kind.'

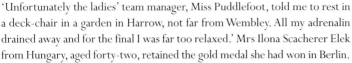

'Unfortunately the ladies' team manager, Miss Puddlefoot, told me to rest in a deck-chair in a garden in Harrow, not far from Wembley. All my adrenalin drained away and for the final I was far too relaxed.' Mrs Ilona Scacherer Elek from Hungary, aged forty-two, retained the gold medal she had won in Berlin.

## GYMNASTICS

Helmut Bantz was the only German involved in the 1948 Olympics. Bantz was a nineteen-year-old Luftwaffe pilot when he was shot down during the Battle of Britain, and in 1948 was still a prisoner of war. He kept fit on a farm in Leicester by digging potatoes and organising sports festivals for his fellow prisoners of war. 'It was so good that even our English guards took part,' he wrote. 'No-one had to be particularly talented. Football was played, one barrack against another. Four ropes were attached to an oak tree to see who could move the fastest hand over hand. We did high jump and long jump and we ran the 100-metre race barefoot across the fields.' Bantz perfected his school English by reading Shakespeare and talking to officials from the Ministry of Food. In early 1948 he was given permission to attend the gymnastics championships in Leicester. He asked if he could go on the horizontal bars, and when the British gymnasts saw him they were amazed. He knew all the moves and was doing them better than they had ever

Ken Buffin from Barry, Wales, executes a flying backroll on the parallel bars at the Empress Hall, Earl's Court. He also competed in the Helsinki and Rome Olympics in 1952 and 1960.

dreamed of. It turned out that before the war he had been coached by a German Olympic gymnast. The British team invited him to be their coach.

'Helmut taught me new manoeuvres and gave us the correct interpretation of the set moves,' said gymnast Frank Turner. 'I received an Olympic uniform,' said Bantz, 'and lived and ate with the British team in the Olympic village. I was asked if I wanted to march with the British team into the stadium. I declined but I had the great pleasure of seeing again many good, old friends in Olympic teams from better days.'

The gymnastics events had been planned for outdoors, but there was so much rain that they were moved to the Empress Hall at Earl's Court. The equipment, brought from several countries, was an odd mixture of different pommel horses and springboards. Britain never expected to win any medals but was pleased to come twelfth out of sixteen national teams.

## AMATEURS

Sport was still socially divided in 1948. Rowing, sailing and fencing were dominated by people who had no need to work, whereas weightlifting and boxing were for those who worked long hours. The amateur rules meant that no-one could accept payment while training or be paid for work connected to their sport. So the oarsman Bert Bushnell had to become a 'marine engineer' because as a 'boat mechanic' he would have been classified as a professional oarsman. Gymnast Frank Turner worked as a film extra and would have been excluded from the games had he performed a single somersault. The Hungarians, Czechoslovaks and Yugoslavs overcame these rules by drafting their top athletes into the army, where they could train all day while being paid as soldiers.

Few British athletes were given days off work for training – they just had to fit in their training in their lunch hours and at weekends. Even the actual Olympic Games were regarded by most employers as an excuse for a holiday.

Jim Halliday of Great Britain was a weightlifter who had to choose his work to fit his hobby. As a schoolboy in 1936 he won the Lancashire weightlifting title. In 1940 his regiment helped to defend Dunkirk, but he was successfully evacuated from Boulogne. In 1941 he was posted to Singapore and, when his ship was bombed, he escaped by jumping on to a ship berthed in the harbour alongside. In 1942 he was captured by the Japanese and spent the next three and a half years as a prisoner of war, working on the notorious Burma–Siam Railway, where fifteen thousand men died of starvation and cholera. When he was released in 1945, he weighed a mere 5 stone. Determined to get fit, he shovelled coal all day at Kearsley power station, and trained at night in a room only inches wider than the bar. Just three years later he was captain of the British Olympic weightlifting team and won a bronze medal. He then became British and Commonwealth champion and broke four weightlifting records.

## ART

Baron de Coubertin died in 1937 but he had always hoped that the revival of the Olympics would create a complete man, developed in both body and mind, through sport *and* art. So artists of all types competed in sculpture, architecture, etchings, poetry and musical composition, on the theme of 'sport'. There were not many entries in any class from Britain – people had all been too busy with the war, and designing sports arenas had been a low priority for British architects. The gold medal for architecture was won by an Austrian architect, Adolf Hoch, for his model of a ski jump. Painting was popular, though many of the pictures depicted activities not featured in the Olympics, such as fishing, children playing and

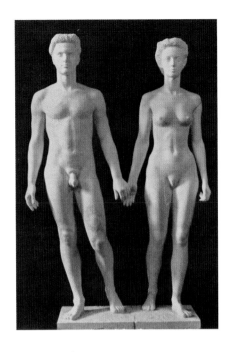

Above: Gustaf Nordhal of Sweden won the gold medal for sculpture with *Homage to Ling*, a full-size nude couple. Ling gymnastics, intended to create beauty of bearing and movement, were demonstrated in Wembley Stadium by four hundred Swedish men and women just before the football final.

Left: An Ovaltine advertisement emphasises the product's role in previous Olympic events.

Programmes from the swimming competition and art exhibition at the 1948 games. New programmes were printed every night with the latest results and different coloured covers.

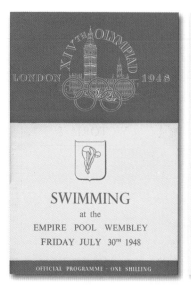

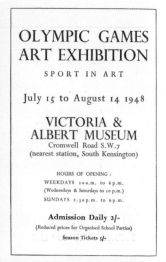

even a race of quagga – an extinct form of zebra. The gold medal for etching was won by a French artist, Albert Decaris, for his homoerotic etching of men at a swimming pool. The critic Pierre Jeannerat wrote, 'It suggests all the delights of water frolics.'

Danish and Swiss judges had to choose between poems written in French, Finnish and Afrikaans. Gilbert Prouteau was a twenty-one-year-old athlete from France who had been injured while training but decided to attend as a spectator. He was surprised when he was told he had won a bronze medal for his poem: 'Rythme du stade' had been submitted without his knowledge. The BBC had offered to judge the music entries and to broadcast the winning compositions, but the standard was considered so lamentable that none of the compositions was heard, let alone broadcast.

The price of tickets ranged from 2s for hockey and horse riding to one guinea for rowing.

Thousands of people paid 2s each to view the entries at the Victoria and Albert Museum in Kensington but 1948 was the last time that artists competed for Olympic medals.

# THE CLOSING CEREMONY

At the closing ceremony fifty thousand people joined together to sing the Olympic Hymn to the tune of 'The Londonderry Air', conducted by Sir Malcolm Sargent. 'Most of us kept our emotions in check until we all sang the closing song,' said weightlifter Maurice Crow from New Zealand. 'It was about going home better people. Not a dry eye in the place after that.'

> The Race is run, the winner wears the laurels,
> But you and I not empty go away;
> For we have seen the least unkind of quarrels,
> The young men glowing in the friendly fray.

> *Refrain:*
> Let us be glad – but not because of winning:
> Let us go home one family today.
> God make our Games a glorious beginning,
> And hand in hand, together guide us on our way.
> If all the lands could run with all the others,
> And work as sweetly as the young men play,
> Lose with a laugh, and battle as brothers,
> Loving to win – but not win every day.

Above: Commemorative stamps totalling 1s 11½d in value. The General Post Office sold 240 million Olympic stamps, worth £3 million.

Below: Olympic officials had to buy their own uniform. This receipt was obtained by Mr S.T. Hurst, chief timekeeper for the swimming events.

The estimate in 1947 for the total cost of putting on the games had been £743,000; the actual expenditure was £732,268 – about £20 million in today's money. After adding up ticket sales, advertising revenue and selling off the sailing dinghies, flags and basketballs, the London organisers surprised everyone with a profit of £29,000. 'The dismal Jimmies who prophesied a failure have been put to rout,' said Sir Arthur Elvin, the chairman of Wembley Stadium.

This was the first international celebration after the Second World War. The indomitable spirit of Londoners cheerfully overcame every obstacle, including shortages of equipment and the worst weather in Olympic history.

'These were the friendliest and least political of all Olympics,' said silver-medal winning high-jumper Dorothy Tyler, the only British athlete to have competed in four Olympics. 'All sports took on a new glow after 1948.'

Despite the bomb sites and the deep economic crisis, the London 1948 games, or 'Austerity Olympics', were among the most successful, inexpensive and unpretentious games of the twentieth century. The traditional four-year cycle of Olympic Games has not been interrupted since 1948.

# WHAT NEXT?

WHAT BECAME of the stars of 1948? Emil Zatopek was promoted to first lieutenant in the Czechoslovakian army and married Dana Ingrova, the gold-medal javelin thrower. In 1952, in Helsinki, Zatopek won gold in the 5,000 metres, 10,000 metres and the marathon – a distance he had never run before. Altogether he broke eighteen world records and was the first man to run 20 km in one hour. In 1968, after speaking out against the Soviet tanks entering Prague, he was forced to work underground as a uranium miner, but when he died in 2000 he was given a state funeral with full honours.

Helmut Bantz met his British friends again when he was a member of the German Olympic gymnastic team in Helsinki in 1952, and at the Melbourne Olympics in 1956, where he won the gold medal for vaulting.

Dame Mary Glen Haig continued fencing into her fifties and became the first British woman to be elected to the IOC.

Almost single-handedly, Fanny Blankers-Koen transformed women's athletics from a sideshow into a central feature of future Olympics. By the time she retired in 1955, Fanny had set sixteen world records in eight different events, and she never lost her realism and generosity. When the American sprinter Marion Jones won three gold medals at Sydney in 2000, Blankers-Koen commented, 'Oh, but she is really good, isn't she? She is training twice a day, we only trained twice a week. I couldn't win four golds today.' Her success matched the record of four gold medals set by Alvin Kraenzlein of the United States in 1900, and equalled by Jesse Owens at Berlin. In December 1999 Blankers-Koen was voted 'Sportswoman of the Century' by the IOC. She died in 2004 at the age of eighty-five.

White City stadium went on to host greyhound racing and speedway but was demolished in 1985 to make way for BBC radio studios. Ten years later a new street in White City was named Dorando Road, after the Italian pastry-maker who had failed to win the marathon in 1908. In 2008 the Westfield shopping complex was opened on the southern end of the original White City site. The same year, not far from White City, the Olympic torch,

Opposite: Londoners in Trafalgar Square erupt with joy at the news that London will host the 2012 Olympic Games, beating four other cities in a close contest.

en route through London to Beijing, was grabbed by a Tibetan protester from the television presenter Konnie Huq.

The Empire Stadium, Wembley, was demolished in 2002 and rebuilt as Wembley Stadium. The Empire Pool became the Wembley Arena and the swimming changing rooms became artistes' dressing rooms. The Beatles, The Who and the Rolling Stones performed to packed and screaming audiences, with the empty pool still beneath the floor.

Each of the London Olympics had its innovations: the 1908 Olympics were the first to be filmed with moving cine cameras, by the Pathé brothers. The 1948 games produced the first full-colour feature documentary, completed in only twenty-six days and shown in cinemas all over Britain. Technical advances in 1948 included starting blocks for sprinters, the photo-finish camera and national television coverage.

The 1948 London games left behind an important social legacy in which sport ceased to be the preserve of gentlemen amateurs: men and women from all backgrounds could join in – and win. Children's comics now featured characters such as Alf Tupper, 'Tough of the Track', who won races on a diet of fish and chips and inspired youngsters that they could do the same if they tried hard enough.

The 1948 Olympics also changed attitudes towards disability. The Stoke Mandeville Games were started in 1948 at the National Spinal Injuries Unit at Aylesbury, with disabled British soldiers competing in archery and wheelchair races. The chief doctor, German-born neurologist Ludwig

Children admire a three-dimensional map of the new Olympic Park in Stratford, London.

Guttmann, believed that sport helped to build up the physical strength and the self-respect of people with disabilities. The International Stoke Mandeville Games began in 1952. Since 1960 the Paralympics have been held in every Olympic year, and since Seoul in 1988 they have taken place at the same venue as the main games.

After 1948 the IOC decided that art at the Olympics would in future be exhibited without the awarding of medals. Although the games have continued to inspire writers, artists and film-makers, 1948 was the last year in which these competitions were held, thus ending Pierre de Coubertin's original concept of the 'whole man'.

London has already twice shown the Olympic movement that the games can be organised at short notice, with little funding. In 2005 London beat Paris in the final round to be chosen by the IOC to host the 2012 games. This is the first time that the same city will have hosted the Olympics three times.

'London is an Olympic winner,' said Jacques Rogge, the President of the IOC. 'I have every confidence that London will host an excellent Games. I met Sebastian Coe in the Olympic Village in Moscow in 1980, just after he had won his gold medal. Who would have thought that we would be where we are today?'

The 2012 London Olympics will take more than a few gentlemen on a committee. It now requires an Act of Parliament, an Olympics Delivery Authority and a London 2012 Organising Committee (still headed by a peer

A computer-generated image by Paul Jennings of the Velopark for the 2012 Olympics. It will be a centre for cyclists of all ages and abilities long after the 2012 Games.

of the realm – Sebastian, now Lord Coe). In 2007 the estimated cost of hosting the games rose from £9 billion to over £22 billion.

The London 2012 Olympics is fast approaching, and the city is working hard to be ready on time. London 2012 has new challenges such as security against terrorism, and the expectation of high standards of arenas, accommodation and transport, for both competitors and spectators. In 1908 and 1948 the government did little to support sport, let alone the Olympics. For 2012, whatever government is in power is expected to contribute out of the public purse.

The first two London Olympics set a high standard for speed and efficiency. 'The new Olympic Park project will regenerate some of the capital's most disadvantaged communities located in east London, which suffered devastating bomb damage during the War,' said Lord Coe.

There will be ten million tickets on sale to people from all over the world. Over fifteen thousand athletes will be staying in and around London, requiring a total 25,000 loaves of bread, 232 tonnes of potatoes, 75,000 litres of milk and 330 tonnes of fruit and vegetables.

It is estimated that over 4.7 billion people – over two-thirds of the world's total population – watched the Beijing Olympics in 2008 on television. By 2012 it is likely to be even more. The BBC has exclusive rights for the United Kingdom, and NBC has already paid over £700 million for the television rights for the United States. That is a big leap from the £20,000 (equivalent to £500,000 today) that J. Arthur Rank paid for the world film rights back in 1948. But then a Mars bar cost only 2d.

# APPENDIX

## PLACES WHERE LONDON OLYMPIC EVENTS WERE HELD

**In 1908**
> Bisley; Clerkenwell; Hurlingham Club; Southampton; Uxendon (nearWembley); White City, Shepherd's Bush; Wimbledon.

**In 1948**
> Aldershot; Bisley; Earl's Court; Empire Stadium, Wembley (now Wembley Stadium); Harringay; Henley-on-Thames; Herne Hill velodrome; Torbay; Empire Pool (now Wembley Arena); Windsor Great Park.

# FURTHER READING

Bannister, Roger. *The First Four Minutes*. Putnam, 1955.

Hampton, Janie. *The Austerity Olympics — When the Games Came to London in 1948*. Aurum, 2008.

Jack, David R. *Matt Busby — My Story*. Souvenir, 1959.

Jenkins, Rebecca. *The First London Olympics 1908*. Piatkus, 2008.

Llewellyn Smith, Michael. *Olympics in Athens 1896: The Invention of the Modern Olympic Games*. Profile, 2004.

Wallechinsky, David. *The Complete Book of the Summer Olympics*. Aurum, 2008.

## WEBSITES
www.topfoto.co.uk/gallery/olympics/1948 – photographs of 1908 and 1948

www.london2012.org – brief history

www.olympics.org – official site of the Olympic movement, with all records

www.sporting-heroes.net – details of results

Diandro Pietri of Italy running the marathon from Windsor Castle towards White City. From *La Dominica Corriere*, August 1908.

# INDEX